Black Therapy

Marlon Stovall (formerly known as Rocky)

Copyright © 2020 Marlon Stovall

All rights reserved.

ISBN: 9798670908733

DEDICATION

My inspiration in this book comes from the recent events that has happened to myself or others whom are Black in America. I want people to know that we have still have a lot to go and racism has still exist and even though one can do all qualifications to not to be a part of a statistic but so man y of us fight every day just for the media to portray us as animals, or threats to the community. So if you are reading this I am pro for myself and my people, as people of color we must make a difference.

CONTENTS

	Acknowledgments	i
1	Dedication to my Readers	1
2	I Am Pro Black	Pg #
3	Black Mama	Pg #
4	Black Az	Pg #
5	That Damn Black Thang	Pg #
6	Black Therapy	Pg #
7	If I Didn't/ Did	Pg #
8	Kinfolk	Pg #
9	Black Weed	Pg #
10	Black Kloud	Pg #

ACKNOWLEDGMENTS

I want to take the time first and foremost and thank God for allowing me the freedom to use my talent and be able to form my words in forms of poems. For a while I was not allowing myself the time and space to take time to work on my craft. I want to thank my mother and friends who encouraged me to keep writing and keep expressing myself on paper. This gives me the encouragement to believe in myself more and realize that this talent should be shared with everyone. I want to thank my mentors in college for pushing me to keep being better then what I was before. Its because of you all that I continued to go to my computer and keeping perfecting my craft.

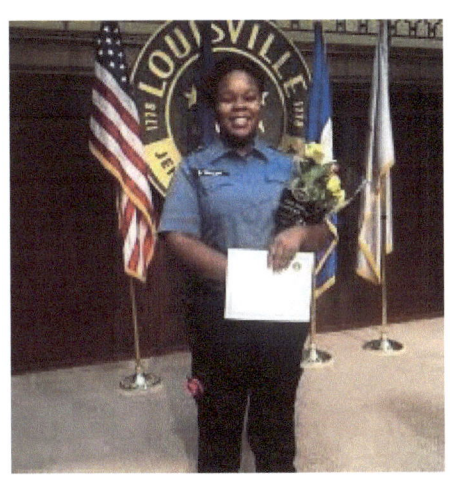

I AM PRO-BLACK

I AM PRO-BLACK, JUST BECAUSE I AM DOESN'T MEAN IM AGAINST YOU, YES YOU SAY ALL LIVES MATTER WELL BLACK LIVES MATTER TOO, TO YOU IM TRYNA EXCLUDE, BUT AT THE SAME TIME WHY DO I HAVE TO VERBALLY SAY THING TO FILL THE VOID, THE WORD "INCLUDE"! MY PRO BLACK IS NOT RUDE, YOU SAY YOU DON'T SEE COLOR BUT DON'T SEE YOUR PRIVELEGE, LETS BOTH DO WRONG YET IM CONVICTED MORE, PUTTING ME OUT IN THE NUDE! I CANT WATER MYSELF DOWN FOR BEING FOR MY PEOPLE, ITS NOT ERASING THE PROBLEM WHEN THE PROBLEM IS NOT SEEING US AS EQUAL! 2020 ITS LIKE THE CIVIL RIGHTS ACT SEQUAL! ALL FOR ONE AND ONE FOR ALL!

IN MY PRO BLACKNESS IM SAYING STAND TOGETHER LETS MAKE ONE CALL! BLACK LIVES MATTER FOR ALL!

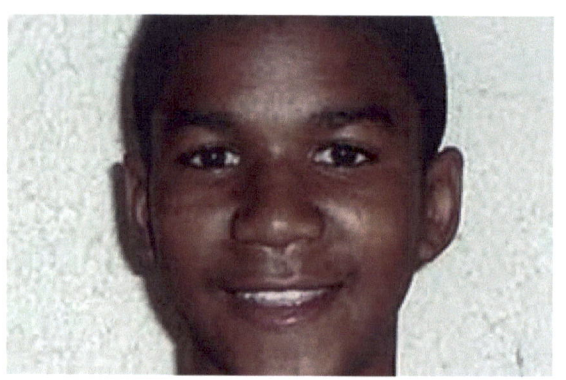

BLACKMAMA

MY BLACK QUEEN THAT WATCHES OVER ME, BIRTHED ME INTO THIS WORLD , GAVE ME THE CHANCE, BELIEVED IN A HIGHER GOD SO I CAN DANCE, GAVE ME AN ENTRANCE ON EARTH, BELIEVED IN THE CHURCH , TAKING MY PAIN WHEN I WAS DOWN AND HURT. TAUGHT ME HOW TO PUSH AND SURVIVE IN THE DIRT! THE BLACK MAMA OF ALL TIME! THE BLACK MAMA THAT GRINDS, THE BLACK MAMA THAT CAN TURN GRAPES INTO WINE, MAKE IT SO FINE, SHE IS THE QUEEN, THE ONE THAT PUTS UP WITH EVERYTHING, THE MAMA OF AFRICA IN MY WORLD, THAT GIRL. BLACK MAMA IS THE

BLACK THERAPY

PROTECTOR THE PROVIDER, THE TEACHER, THE OVERSEER, WE BE A FOOL TO NOT PUT FAITH IN HER!

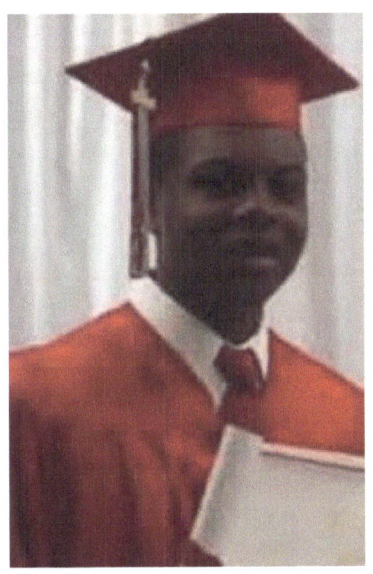

BLACK AZ

BLACK AZ A PANTHER THAT LURKS BEYOND THE BLACK NIGHT, BLACK AZ A ROPE THE

THINGS THAT CAN LOCK IN A KNOT , THE STRENGTH OF OUR DREADLOCKS, BLACK AZ MY MELANIN, THE ONE YOU SEE AZ A SIN , BUT WITHIN MY BLACK AZZ KNOW WHAT IM CABLE OF KNOWING IM IN IT FOR THE WIN! TAKE MY CULTURE AND GIVE IT A SPIN BECAUSE BABY YOU WANT IN! MY BLACK AZZ IS NOT A FASHION, WANTING THE BIG LIPS FOR THE CUSHION , THE SWAY IN THE MOTION OF THE OCEAN, THE STRENGTH OF AN OX, SEPARATE US YET STILL PUT US IN A BOX, MY BLACK

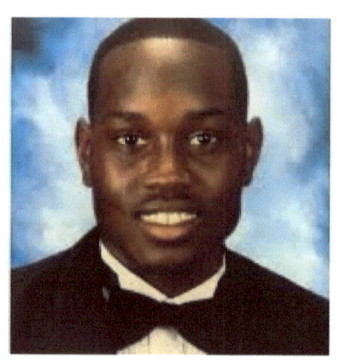

THAT DAMN BLACK THANG

WE ARE THAT DAMN BLACK THING WHEN THEY WANT TO ADOPT OUR DIALECT! THEY SPEAK IN OUR SLANG, BUT WHEN IT COMES TO BLACK LIVES MATTER SOME HAVEN'T SAID A DAMN THANG! WE YOU WERE BUMPING HARD TO OUR AFRICAN ROOTS, YOU STARTED TO LOOT US WHEN YOU HID BEHIND YOUR RACISM. OH THE NEWS SAID HE WAS A THUG, BUT I ASK YOU WHAT IF IT WAS ME? ITS JUST BECAUSE YOU LAUGH AND SHRUG BECAUSE I WASN'T YOUR PERCEPTION AS GHETTO! I STAND BEHIND THAT COULD'VE EASILY BEEN ME! YOU ADOPT OUR CULTURE SHUT TO RIP UP THE SCRIPTURES! YOU WANT THAT DAMN BLACK THANG, WANTING SO BAD TO HANG! COP KILLS BLACK MAN BANG BANG, YOU SAY ITS INSANE, WELL STEP UP AND SAY THEIR NAMES! LET ME THEM KNOW THAT TRULY EVERYBODY IS THE SAME! THEY WANTED THAT BLACK THUG FOR THE CASH BUT WHEN IT ALL BOILED DOWN TO STEPPING UP, YOU TURN AROUND AND SHOW ME YOUR!

BLACK THERAPY

WE ARE SUFFERING IN SILENCE! PLEASE GET THE HELP THAT YOU NEED! IT'S TOTALLY OKAY TO SEEK A PERSON THAT CAN HELP YOU GAIN
THE POWER AND LEAD! PLEASE GET THE HELP YOU NEED! BATTLING WITH THE OPPRESSORS, TRYING TO STEP UP IN LIFE TO BUILD ON MY LIFE BETTER! SEPARATION AND DEPRESSION, OPRESSION, CLASSIFICATIONS AS A MINORITIES WE ARE ON THE LOWEST ON THE POLE. I KNOW
IT'S SO COLD BUT THIS IS ROLE! WE STRUGGLE TO BREAK THROUGH THE HATE AMONGST OUR OWN VERSUS THE HATRED OF THE NON-POV OPPOSITES! WE JUST NOW BEGAN TO BE ABLE TO HAVE A SEAT AT THE SAME TABLE, BUT WHEN I TURN ON THE CABLE EVERYDAY WITH MY EYE LENSE, I FEEL FOR THE STRUGGLE OF MY PEOPLE! WE WANT TO BE COME ONE WITH THEM BUT YET WE DON'T ALWAYS SEE EACH OTHER AS EQUAL! WHAT ARE WE DOING TO OURSELVES THAT ITS HARD TO LOVE EACH OTHER, NOW THEY ATTEMPTING TO ERASE OUR CULTURE! FUCKIN DAMN VULTURES! ITS JUST NOW WE NEED TO DO WHATS BEST FOR US MENTALLY BEFORE WE EVENTUALLY RUPTURE!

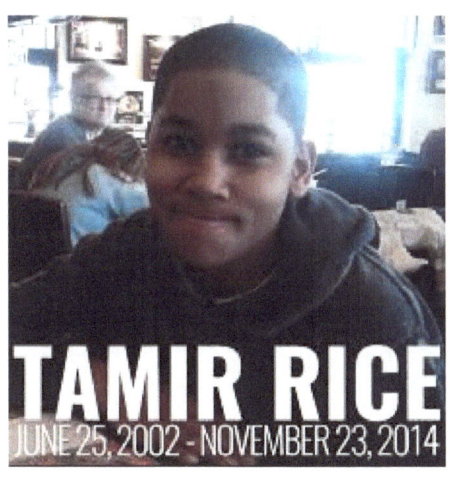

IF I DIDN'T /DID (DEDICATED TO MY SLAIN BROTHAS AND SISTAS)

IF I DIDN'T MAKE ME IT THROUGH BY YOUR RULES WOULD THAT MAKE ME A FAILURE, IF I DIDN'T HAVE THE MEANS TO MAKE SOMETHING OUT OF MYSELF BY YOUR STATISTICAL DATA WOULD THAT PUT ME AT RISK FOR DANGER. IF NOBODY WOULDA HIRED ME AND I HAD TO FIND WAYS TO HUSTLE TO FEED MYSELF AND FAMILY WOULD I BE YOUR AMUSE TO PICK ON ME AND THROW ME IN YOUR JAIL CELLAR. IF I DIDN'T SPEAK PROPERLY IN YOUR MIND WOULD YOU SAY IM A DUMB NIGGA? IF I MIND MY BUSINESS WOULD YOU SAY I WAS SCARY BECAUSE I WAS DARKER HUE AND THE FACT IM BIGGER? YOU WONDER

WHY I ASK THESE QUESTIONS AND NOW DAYS IT SEEM LIKE THE HUMAN NATURE. IM JUST TRYING TO LIVE MY LIFE TO STAY OUT YOUR WAY. LIVING IN FEAR INSIDE MY HEAD DAY AFTER DAY. I DON'T WANT TO BE AT THE HANDS OF THE PERSON WHO CAN HAVE ME HANG. I DON'T WANT TO BE ON THE NEWS FOR MY FAMILY AND FRIENDS TO FIND OUT IVE BEEN SLAIN. YOU SAY RACISM DOESN'T EXIST YET TO SEE MY PEOPLE STILL FACE THIS CAUSES ME SO MUCH PAIN. I JUST WANT TO LIVE MY LIFE SIMPLE AND PLAIN. PRAYING TO GOD TO LIVE ANOTHER DAY. MY FELLOW HUMANS WHY MUST IT BE THIS WAY! DYING OVER CD'S SELLING, SKITTLES PURCHASING, RUNNING TRAFFIC LIGHTS, AND CANT ESCAPE THE HANDS OF YOU WITH OUT A FIGHT, AND I FIGHT AND FIGHT, YOU BEAT ME UNTIL I LOSE BREATH AND VIEW THE BLACK SIDE OF MY EYE SIGHT. IN HEAVEN I BECAUSE YOU TAKEN MY LIFE! PRAYING TO GOD TO PROTECT MY FAMILY AND PROTECT MY FUTURE SONS FROM THE THIEVES OF THE NIGHT. THIS JUST AINT RIGHT MAKES ME WANT TO CRY, WE WANT TO LIVE BUT THE HANDS OF OUR ENEMIES APPLYING PRESSURE TO OUR NECKS, HAND CUFFED TIGHT! THIS IS NOT RIGHT! BLUE LIVES WHY! STOP CUTTING OFF MY BLACK LIFE! I JUST WANT TO LIVE AND NOT DIE!

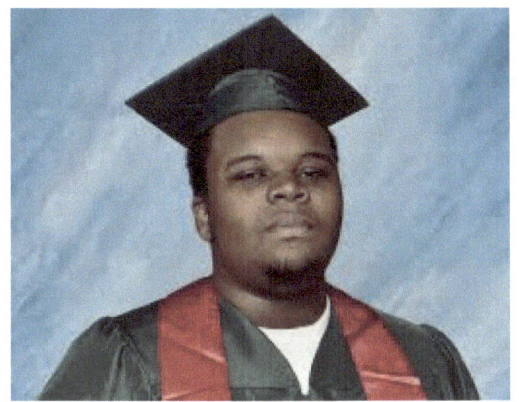

KINFOLK

I LOVE MY KIN FOLK LIKE THE DAYS WHEN WE PLAY MARVIN GAYE DOING THE TIMES WITH DRINKS, POPS ON THE BARBECUE , WHILE MY SIBLINGS AND COUSINS PULL OUT THE CARDS PLAYING SPADES. WE LAUGH AND GET DOWN THE PARTY LINE, HENNESSY , COKE AND WINE, YES A DAMN FINE TIME WITH THIS BLACK FAMILY OF MINE. FUSSING OVER WHO MADE THE POTATO SALAD, YES WE LAUGH AT OUR OWN KIND , WHEN THEY FIND OUT WHO COOKED THE SOUL FOOD MEALS DURING DINNER TIME. HOW I MISS THE CHILLED UNCLES WITH CIGS, GETTING DOWN WITH CHICAGO , KELLY AND MR. BIGGS. OH THE BOUNDING OF THE TIME. WHEN YOUR AUNTIE CLAIMS SHE DOESN'T EAT THE SMOKED SWINE. THE GOSSIP ABOUT WHOSE CHILDREN ARE THE WORSE, AND YET WE GET MAD AT WHOMEVER THROWS THE PUNCHES FIRST, SOMEONE HAD WAY TO MUCH LIQUOR, WHILE THE CHILDREN SCREAM AND KICK, YOUR YOUNGER TEENAGE BAD ASS COUSINS THINKING THEY GROWN , HIDING IN THE BACK ROOM , PROVING THEY'VE GROWN BY EVERY CURSE WORD. WHEN YOUR MAMA AND AUNTS WALK PAST SAYING " UMMM DID I JUST HEAR WHAT I HEARD". EMBARRASED BECAUSE YOU MEANT TO BE GROWN, MAKING YOUR VOICE LOWER. MY KINFOLK WAS ARE THE BOND LIKE NAPS IN OUR HAIR TO FORM THESE BRAIDS, WHILE YOUR SISTER BRUSHES HER DAUGHTER THICK HAIR, USING HOT IRONS TO GIVE IT FLARE.

EATING THAT GOOD MACARONI AND CHEESE, CHICKEN AND ALL KIND OF BEANS, THESE ARE WHY US KINFOLK GET TOGETHER BECAUSE WE KNOW WHAT TRUE FAMILY MEANS. CATCHING UP ON EVERYTHING IN HOPES TO SEE THAT FACE THE NEXT SCENE. NO THOUGHTS OF FUNERALS , LOUD LAUGHTER WHILE IN THE BACKYARD SMOKING THAT GREEN. CAN WE GO BACK TO THAT KINFOLK DREAM!

BLACK WEED (ODE TO MENTAL HEALTH)

CAN BURN IT UNTIL IT TURN TO ASHES, YALL NOT HEARING ME THOUGH, WHEN THIS WORLD IS HURTING ME I JUST GOT TO RELEASE JUST GOTTA LET IT GO, NO I DON'T WANT TO FEEL THIS NO MORE, SEE THIS NO MORE, I WANT MY MENTAL PROBLEMS OUT THE DOOR! BLACK, THEY WANT TO KILL ME, GAY BECAUSE THEY DON'T EVEN SEE, DISABLED TIRED OF TRYING TO BE POSITIVE, GET OUT MY HEAD, TIRED FLIPPIN ON THE GOT DAMN NEWS, TIRED OF SEEING MY PEOPLE DEAD, BUT YOU NEVER HEAR ME THOUGH, LET ME JUST GET HIGHER AND HIGHER UNTIL I CANT FEEL THIS IS NOT REALITY ,THIS JUST ISN'T REAL. IM QUIET WHILE IM SUFFERING IN SILENCE, NOT FEELING MYSELF AT THIS MOMENT, I WANT TO BETTER AND GREATER JUST CLIMB THIS LADDER. BUT I FALL AND ALL. WHY AM I ALWAYS SECOND GUESSING MYSELF, WANTING TO CHASE LOVE, BUT LOVE DON'T CHASE ME, TIRED OF ASKING IF I AM WORTHY. SO I SMOKE THIS WEED, TO LET OUT SOME STEAM, I DON'T WANT TO BE ANY BODIES MAINSTREAM DREAMZ. I JUST WANT TO GET AWAY , AWAY SOMETIMES, LET ME COOL OFF YES ILL BE FINE. COVID GOT ME GOING CRAZY, I WANT TO LIVE MY LIFE LATELY, THEY SAY WE ARE AT THE TOP OF LIST, CANNOT I FIND A WATER WELL WITH SOME MAGIC, GOT I CANT SEEM TO HANDLE IT. GOT ME LOOKING AT MYSELF IN THE MIRROR. I DON'T WANT TO BITTER, BUT THE WORLD HAS

SHOWN ME, THAT SNAKES SLITHER, I AM JUST WORKING EVERYDAY STRIVING TO BE A WINNER. I JUST WANT THE WORLD TO GET BETTER. LIVE A LITTLER GREATER, RAISE ABOVE MY HATERS. WHY YOU JUST LET ME BE, TIRED OF PEOPLE HURTING ME. WHY CANT YOU SEE THAT YOU MAKE ME MEAN. WELL MAYBE ITS WHOSE IN BREATHING IN MY AIR UNCOMFORTABLY. WHO AM I? WHY MUST I ASK MYSELF THESE QUESTION WHEN I KNOW I'M BLESSING BUT IM NOT INNOCENT. BUT PLEASE JUST LET ME BE, I DON'T WANT NOBODY ELSE HURTING ME.

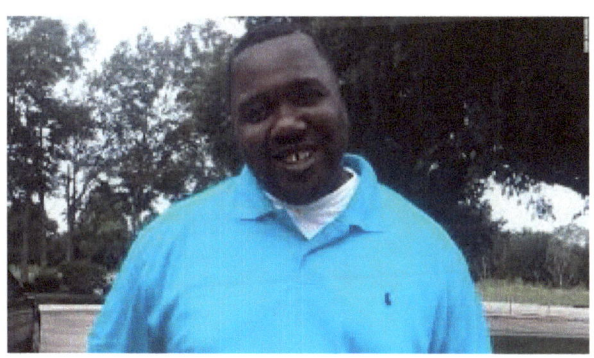

BLACK KLOUD

I JUST DON'T WANT TO BE LOOKED AT AS A BLACK CLOUD, THE ONE THAT HOVERS OVER, WITH THUNDEROUS SOUNDS, HAILING OVER THE HEADS OF ONES THAT FRUSTRATES ME. I WAS ONCE THE SUNNY DAYS, UNTIL YOUR WORLD WINDS BROUGHT THE SWAY OF THE WEATHER IS BIPOLAR WAYS. I AM THE FALL , THE TORNADO, THE SPRING THE WINTER , AND RAIN. IM NOT YOUR PERFECT HURRICANE. TRYING TO CONTROL THE WINDS STABLE AND SANE. BLACK KLOUD IS WHAT THE WEATHERMAN CLAIMS TO BE THE ANGRY, BLACK MAN. DON'T SHOW YOUR EMOTIONS, BUT HAVE LESS MOTION. AS IF THE WATER NEVER HITS THE RIFTS AND DROWNS THE SHORE OF THE OCEAN. DON'T SHOW YOUR EMOTIONS, BUT HAVE LESS EMOTION. CONTROL YOUR EMOTIONS. IGNORE THE PROVOKING DON'T IN MOVE IN CERTAIN MOTION. BUT BLACK MAN CONTROL YOUR EMOTIONS!!! THEY FORGET WE WERE HUMAN, THE ATMOSPHERE CREATES THE FORMING OF THE BLACK CLOUD FORMATION. TAUGHT TO BE HARD, DON'T SMILE, BUT YET WE INTIMIDATING. SUNNY DAYS SUDDENLY FADING. BLACK CLOUDS HOVER OVER , WHILE THE FIRE IN THE SKY IS SHADING. CREATING THE ATMOSPHERE OF A BLACK MALE, TELLING US WE SHOULD SHINE WHILE THE RAINING IS

POURING, ACKNOWLEDGE US HOW YOU WOULD DO YOUR OWN, NOT JUST HIDING BY HIDING IN THE NIGHT, BUT ACKNOWLEDGE OUR BEING AS LOUD IN THE MORNING.

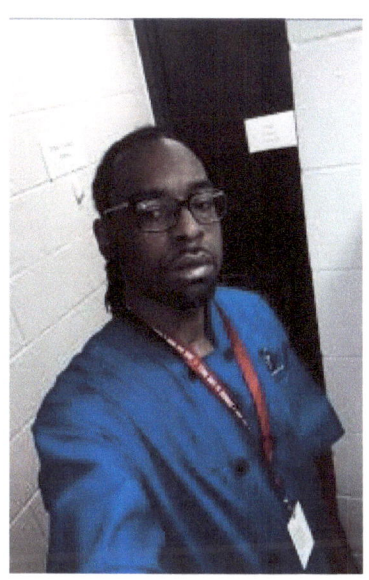

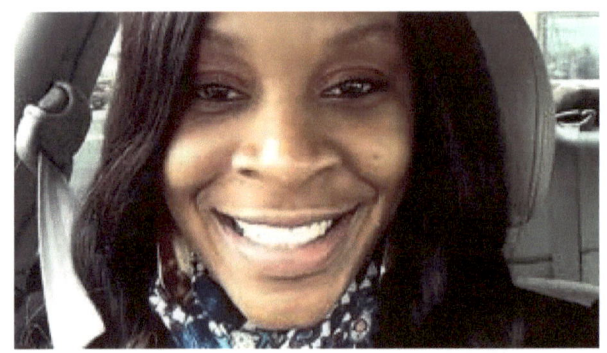

ABOUT THE AUTHOR

Marlon Stovall better known as Rocky, the author of Trapped In A Thing We Call Love, Stages of Perseverance, and Rebirth, and now Black Therapy, among other works, lives in Chicago, IL but born in Justice, IL was born to two parents Essie and Wayne Stovall and the youngest of two older siblings have always had dreams to shine and achieve his goals. A Former Southern Illinois University-Carbondale student with a Bachelor's Of Science and Social Worked learned a lot about living life as African American, Disabled male. Inspired by recent events in the media pertaining to minorities he has created a collection of poems expressing his observations and personal feelings in the world. The book is for my people and people who are for my people.

www.ingramcontent.com/pod-product-compliance
Lightning Source LLC
Chambersburg PA
CBHW040350220526
45473CB00009B/2842